COPYRIGHT © 2004 Nanci Bell
Gander Publishing
412 Higuera Street, Suite 200
San Luis Obispo, CA 93401
805-541-5523 • 800-554-5523

VISUALIZING AND VERBALIZING IS A REGISTERED TRADEMARK OF NANCI BELL

All rights reserved. No part of this material shall be reproduced or transmitted in any form or by any means, electronic or mechanical, including photocopying, recording, or by any information or retrieval system, without prior written permission from the Publisher. Printed in the U.S.A.

ISBN 0-945856-37-7

Overview and Directions

This workbook is designed to develop gestalt imagery and language comprehension with the Visualizing and Verbalizing for Language Comprehension and Thinking® (V/V®) Program.

Following the steps of V/V®, detail and gestalt imagery are developed with Sentence by Sentence, Multiple Sentence, Whole Paragraph, and Paragraph by Paragraph V/V® stimulation.

Each story is high in imagery and followed by these workbook activities:

- Imagery Questions
- Picture Summary
- Word Summary
- Main Idea
- Higher Order Thinking Skills (HOTS)
- Paragraph Writing

As the student begins each story, he/she should decode the vocabulary words and visualize the meaning. This will help create imagery and develop contextual fluency. The student may write phrases or partial sentences to describe his/her imagery.

These workbooks have been written specifically to help students learn and discover the wonder of the written word by improving gestalt imagery, critical thinking, and writing skills. Once these skills are developed, the possibilities are endless.

Remember, you can help students do this. You can do anything!

Nanci Bell
2004

There are three workbooks at each reading level:

Book 1 • Sentence by Sentence
Book 2 • Sentence by Sentence and Multiple Sentence
Book 3 • Multiple Sentence, Whole Sentence, and Paragraph by Paragraph

Meet Ivan!

I am Ivan, King of the Neighborhood. I'm big and wide and full of pride!	I **love** to eat!
I **love** to sleep! 	I am a cat!

1 The Flat Fish

Sentence by Sentence
Date: _____

The sole is a flat fish that can change color to match his surroundings. He has both eyes on one side of his body and lies flat on the bottom of the sea. Then he changes color to match the sand. This way, he can hide from his enemies and still look around. If he is put on a chessboard, he can even change to match the black and white squares.

Vocabulary:

sole: a type of flat fish that lies on the bottom of the ocean
surroundings: the area around something
chessboard: a board with black and white squares that is used to play chess

1 First Sentence: The sole is a flat fish that can change color to match his surroundings.

What did those words make you picture? _____
_____
_____

1. What did you picture for the sole? _____
_____

2. What did you see for him changing color? _____
_____

3. What colors did you picture? _____
_____

4. How did you see his surroundings? _____
_____

2 Second Sentence: He has both eyes on one side of his body and lies flat on the bottom of the sea.

What did those words make you picture? _____
_____
_____

1. What did you picture for the sole's eyes? _____
_____

2. On what part of his body did you picture his eyes? _____
_____

3. How many eyes did you picture on one side of the sole? _____
_____

4. What did you see for him lying on the bottom of the sea? _____
_____

3 Third Sentence: Then he changes color to match the sand.

What did those words make you picture? _____
_____
_____

1. What did you picture for the color of the sand? _____
_____

2. What color did you see him changing from and to? _____
_____

3. What did you see for him matching the sand? _____
_____

4. Did you picture this up close or from far away? _____
_____

4 Fourth Sentence: This way, he can hide from his enemies and still look around.

What did those words make you picture? _____
_____
_____

1. What did you picture for his enemies? _____
_____

2. What did you see the sole doing when an enemy came close? _____
_____

3. What did you see an enemy doing when it came near a sole? _____
_____

4. What did you see for the sole looking around? _____
_____

5 Fifth Sentence: If he is put on a chessboard, he can even change to match the black and white squares.

What did those words make you picture? _____
_____
_____

1. What did you picture for a chessboard? _____
_____

2. What did you see for the squares on the chessboard? _____
_____

3. What colors did you picture the sole becoming? _____
_____

Picture Summary:

Number your images in order.

☐ The sole can hide from his enemies and still look around.

☐ If the sole is put on a chessboard, he can even change to match the black and white squares.

☐ The sole is a flat fish that has both his eyes on one side of his body.

☐ The sole can change his color to match his surroundings.

Critical Thinking

Write a Word Summary:

_____
_____
_____
_____
_____

Main Idea:

Check the box that best describes all your images—the main idea.

☐ The sole is a fish that has both eyes on one side of his body.

☐ The sole is a fish that has eyes on one side of his body and can change colors to match his surroundings.

☐ The sole can change his colors to match the squares of a chessboard.

HOTS Questions:

1. Why do you think the sole changes color to match his surroundings? _____
_____

2. Why do you think he lies flat on the bottom of the sea? _____
_____

3. Why do you think he is called a flat fish? _____
_____

4. Why do you think he has eyes on only one side of his body? _____
_____

5. Why might it be good for both of his eyes to be on one side of his body? _____
_____

6. Why do you think he might need to look around when lying at the bottom of the sea? _____
_____

Write a Story

Make up a story about anything you want!

_____
_____
_____
_____
_____
_____
_____
_____
_____
_____
_____
_____
_____
_____
_____
_____

Did you use all the Structure Words in your story? Check each one you used.

What	Size	Color	Mood	Background	Perspective
Number	Shape	Movement	Where	When	Sound

2 Lifesaving Dog

The huge St. Bernard dog ran easily through the deep mountain snow. Moving very quickly, the brown and white dog searched for the lost skier. Within moments, she found the skier lying half-buried under the snow. After licking the skier's face to wake him up, she lay down around him to keep him warm. Then she barked and barked for the rescuers to come.

Sentence by Sentence
Date: _____

Vocabulary:

St. Bernard dog: a type of dog that is very large and strong
skier: a person who skis
rescuers: people who save others from danger

---

1 First Sentence: The huge St. Bernard dog ran easily through the deep mountain snow.

What did those words make you picture? _____
_____
_____

1. What did you picture for the St. Bernard dog? _____
_____

2. What did you see for how the dog was moving in the snow? _____
_____

3. Where did you see this happening? _____
_____

4. What did you see for the deep snow? _____
_____

---

2 Second Sentence: Moving very quickly, the brown and white dog searched for the lost skier.

What did those words make you picture? _____
_____
_____

1. What color did you picture the St. Bernard? _____
_____

2. How did you see her moving—fast or slow? _____
_____

3. What did you see for her searching? _____
_____

4. What did you see for the skier? _____
_____

3. Third Sentence: Within moments, she found the skier lying half-buried under the snow.

What did those words make you picture? _____

_____

1. What did you see for her finding the skier? _____

_____

2. What did you picture for where the skier was? _____

_____

3. How did you see "half-buried" under the snow? _____

_____

4. Were you seeing this up close or from far away? _____

_____

4. Fourth Sentence: After licking the skier's face to wake him up, she lay down around him to keep him warm.

What did those words make you picture? _____

_____

1. What did you see for the St. Bernard licking his face? _____

_____

2. What did you picture for her tongue? _____

_____

3. What did you see for her lying down around him? _____

_____

4. What did you see for her keeping the skier warm? _____

_____

5. Fifth Sentence: Then she barked and barked for the rescuers to come.

What did those words make you picture? _____

_____

1. What did you see for the St. Bernard barking? _____

_____

2. What movement did you see for her tail as she barked? _____

_____

3. What sounds did you hear? _____

Picture Summary:

Number your images in order.

☐ After licking the skier's face to wake him up, she lay down around him to keep him warm.

☐ The St. Bernard dog ran easily through the snow searching for the lost skier.

☐ Then the dog barked and barked for the rescuers to come.

☐ Within moments, the St. Bernard dog found the skier half-buried under the snow.

Critical Thinking

Write a Word Summary:

_____

_____

_____

_____

Main Idea:

Check the box that best describes all your images—the main idea.

- [ ] The St. Bernard dog found the lost skier and kept him warm for the rescuers.

- [ ] The St. Bernard dog found the lost skier half-buried under the snow.

- [ ] The St. Bernard dog licked the skier's face to wake him up.

HOTS Questions:

1. Why do you think the huge St. Bernard dog could move easily in the snow? _____

2. How do you think she was able to find the lost skier? _____

3. Why do you think she licked the skier's face? _____

4. Do you think the St. Bernard dog had a loud bark or a soft bark? _____

5. Do you think it took a long time for rescuers to find the skier? Explain. _____

6. Why do you think these St. Bernard dogs are used for rescue missions in the snow? _____

Write a Story

Make up an exciting story about a St. Bernard dog and a dangerous rescue high on a mountain.

Did you use all the Structure Words in your story? Check each one you used.

What	Size	Color	Mood	Background	Perspective
Number	Shape	Movement	Where	When	Sound

3 The Pink Dolphin

Sentence by Sentence
Date: _____

Rare pink dolphins live in some lakes and rivers in South America. The water is muddy, so they have small eyes and poor eyesight. Instead, they have very long noses with stiff hairs on them. The hairs help the dolphins feel what is around them.

Vocabulary:

rare: hard to find
pink dolphins: a type of dolphin that lives in fresh water and not salt water like most dolphins
South America: a large continent that is south of North America
eyesight: being able to see

---

1 **First Sentence:** Rare pink dolphins live in some lakes and rivers in South America.

What did those words make you picture? _____
_____
_____

1. What did you picture for the dolphins? _____
   _____

2. What color did you picture them? _____
   _____

3. Where did you picture them living—in the ocean or lakes and rivers?
   _____

4. What did you picture for South America? _____
   _____

---

2 **Second Sentence:** The water is muddy, so they have small eyes and poor eyesight.

What did those words make you picture? _____
_____
_____

1. What did you see for the muddy water? _____
   _____

2. Did you picture a lake or a river? _____
   _____

3. What did you picture for the dolphin's eyes? _____
   _____

4. What did you see for them having "poor eyesight?" _____
   _____

3 **Third Sentence:** Instead, they have very long noses with stiff hairs on them.

What did those words make you picture? _____
_____
_____

1. What did you see for their long noses? _____
_____

2. What size did you see their noses? _____
_____

3. What did you see for the stiff hairs? _____
_____

4. Did you see those hairs from up close or from far away? _____
_____

4 **Fourth Sentence:** The hairs help the dolphins feel what is around them.

What did those words make you picture? _____
_____
_____

1. How did you see the nose hairs helping the dolphins? _____
_____

2. What did you see around the dolphins? _____
_____

3. Were you seeing this up close or from far away? _____
_____

4. What sounds did you hear? _____
_____

Picture Summary:

Number your images in order.

- ▉ The water is muddy, so pink dolphins have poor eyesight.

- ▉ The hairs on their noses help dolphins feel what is around them.

- ▉ Rare pink dolphins live in some lakes and rivers in South America.

- ▉ Pink dolphins have very long noses with stiff hairs on them.

Write a Word Summary:

_____
_____
_____
_____
_____
_____
_____

Critical Thinking

Main Idea:

Check the box that best describes all your images—the main idea.

☐ Pink dolphins have the perfect body for the lakes and rivers where they live.

☐ The pink dolphins have small eyes and poor eyesight.

☐ Pink dolphins have long noses with stiff hairs that help them feel around.

HOTS Questions:

1. Why do you think pink dolphins are rare? _____
_____

2. Why do you think they might be pink? _____
_____

3. What affect do you think muddy water has on the size of their eyes? _____
_____

4. Why do you think they have poor eyesight? _____
_____

5. Do you think they need good eyesight? Why or why not? _____
_____

6. Why do you think they have long noses? _____
_____

7. How do you think their stiff nose hairs help them? _____
_____

Write a Story

Make up a story about an adventure and seeing a pink dolphin.

_____

_____

_____

_____

_____

_____

_____

_____

_____

_____

_____

_____

_____

_____

Did you use all the Structure Words in your story? Check each one you used.

What	Size	Color	Mood	Background	Perspective
Number	Shape	Movement	Where	When	Sound

4 Land of the Light

Sentence by Sentence
Date: _____

Finland, a country in the far north, is covered in snow from fall to spring and is dark a lot of the time. But when summer comes, the sun never goes down in this cold place. There is sunlight for at least two and a half months, even at night. People have to keep their shades pulled down or wear sleep masks so they can sleep at night!

Vocabulary:

Finland: a country in the northern part of Europe

far north: the cold northern part of the world, near the Arctic Circle

---

1 First Sentence: Finland, a country in the far north, is covered in snow from fall to spring and is dark a lot of the time.

What did those words make you picture? _____
_____
_____

1. What did you picture for where Finland is? _____
_____

2. What did you picture for the weather in Finland? _____
_____

3. How many months did you see from fall to spring? _____
_____

4. What did you see for it being dark a lot? _____
_____

---

2 Second Sentence: But when summer comes, the sun never goes down in this cold place.

What did those words make you picture? _____
_____
_____

1. What did you picture for summer? _____
_____

2. What did you see for summer coming? _____
_____

3. What did you picture for the sun never going down? _____
_____

4. What did you picture for nighttime in the summer? _____
_____

3 Third Sentence: There is sunlight for at least two and a half months, even at night.

What did those words make you picture? _____
_____
_____

1. What did you see for sunlight? _____
_____

2. How long did you see the sunlight lasting? _____
_____

3. What did you picture for night? _____
_____

4. Were you picturing this up close or from far away? _____

4 Fourth Sentence: People have to keep their shades pulled down or wear sleep masks so they can sleep at night!

What did those words make you picture? _____
_____
_____

1. What did you see for people pulling their shades down? _____
_____

2. What did you picture for a sleep mask? _____
_____

3. What did you see for someone sleeping with a mask on? _____
_____

4. What did you see people doing when they tried to sleep without the shades down or a sleep mask?
_____

Picture Summary:

Number your images in order.

☐ In Finland, there is snow from fall to spring.

☐ People have to keep their shades pulled down or wear sleep masks so they can sleep at night!

☐ When summer comes, the sun never goes down in this cold place.

☐ There is sunlight for at least two and a half months, even at night.

Write a Word Summary:

_____
_____
_____
_____
_____
_____
_____

Critical Thinking

Main Idea:

Check the box that best describes all your images—the main idea.

☐ The sun shines all the time during the summer in Finland.

☐ People wear sleep masks in Finland.

☐ Finland is covered in snow from fall to spring.

HOTS Questions:

1. Why do you think Finland is covered in snow so much of the year? _____

2. How is the summer different in Finland than where you live? _____

3. How do you think people can tell the difference between night and day? _____

4. Why do you think people might have trouble sleeping? _____

5. What do you think people might do to get some sleep? _____

6. What do you think might be good about it being light all night? _____

7. How would you feel if it were light all day and all night? _____

Write a Story

Make up a story about living in Finland.

Did you use all the Structure Words in your story? Check each one you used.

What	Size	Color	Mood	Background	Perspective
Number	Shape	Movement	Where	When	Sound

5 Robots and Sheep

Two men in Australia came up with the idea for a robot that cuts the white wool off of sheep. The sheep is put into a sort of cloth cradle that holds it in place safely. A robot arm with clippers at the end cuts the wool off. The wool falls onto a moving belt and is taken away to be cleaned. The system is fast and never hurts or scares the sheep.

Sentence by Sentence
Date: _____

Vocabulary:

Australia: an island country in the southern part of the world
cradle: a frame that is used to hold something
clippers: a tool that is used to cut hair or wool

---

1 First Sentence: Two men in Australia came up with the idea for a robot that cuts the white wool off of sheep.

What did those words make you picture? _____

_____

_____

1. What did you see for the men? _____

_____

2. What did you picture for how they came up with the idea? _____

_____

3. What did you see for the sheep? _____

_____

4. What color did you picture for the wool on the sheep? _____

_____

---

2 Second Sentence: The sheep is put into a sort of cloth cradle that holds it in place safely.

What did those words make you picture? _____

_____

_____

1. What did you picture for the cradle? _____

_____

2. What did you see for the sheep being put in the cradle? _____

_____

3. What did you picture for the cloth of the cradle? _____

_____

4. What did you see for the cradle holding the sheep safely? _____

_____

3 **Third Sentence:** A robot arm with clippers at the end cuts the wool off.

What did those words make you picture? _____
_____
_____

1. What did you see for a robot arm? _____
_____

2. What did you picture for clippers? _____
_____

3. What did you see for the clippers cutting the wool off? _____
_____

4. What did you see for the wool coming off the sheep? _____
_____

4 **Fourth Sentence:** The wool falls onto a moving belt and is taken away to be cleaned.

What did those words make you picture? _____
_____
_____

1. What did you see for where the wool fell? _____
_____

2. What did you see for the moving belt? _____
_____

3. How fast did you picture the belt moving? _____
_____

4. Did you picture the wool as clean or dirty? _____
_____

5 **Fifth Sentence:** The system is fast and never hurts or scares the sheep.

What did those words make you picture? _____
_____
_____

1. What did you picture for the system? _____
_____

2. What did you picture for fast? _____
_____

3. What sounds did you hear? _____
_____

Picture Summary:

Number your images in order.

☐ A robot arm with clippers at the end cuts the wool off.

☐ The sheep is placed in a cloth cradle.

☐ Two men in Australia came up with the idea for a robot that cuts the white wool off of sheep.

☐ The wool falls onto a moving belt and is taken away to be cleaned.

Critical Thinking

Write a Word Summary:

_____
_____
_____
_____
_____
_____

Main Idea:

Check the box that best describes all your images—the main idea.

☐ Two men invented a robot that can cut the wool off sheep safely and quickly.

☐ The wool falls onto a moving belt and is taken away to be cleaned.

☐ The robot arm has clippers on the end to cut the wool off the sheep.

HOTS Questions:

1. Why do you think the two men wanted to invent a robot to cut the wool off sheep? _____
_____

2. Why do you think the sheep needs to be held in a cradle? _____
_____

3. Why do you think the cradle was made of cloth and not metal? _____
_____

4. Why do you think the wool falls onto a moving belt? _____
_____

5. Why do you think the robot might be better than a person at cutting wool? _____
_____

6. What do you think happens to the wool after it is cleaned? _____
_____

Write a Story

Make up a story about going to Australia and helping to cut the wool off of the sheep.

_____
_____
_____
_____
_____
_____
_____
_____
_____
_____
_____
_____
_____
_____

Did you use all the Structure Words in your story? Check each one you used.

What	Size	Color	Mood	Background	Perspective
Number	Shape	Movement	Where	When	Sound

6 The Fastest Cat

Sentence by Sentence
Date: _____

The cheetah, a large spotted cat from Africa, is the fastest animal in the world. With his long powerful legs and slender body, he can run up to 70 miles an hour. But he can only run this fast for a short time. So the cheetah sneaks through the tall grass looking for a small antelope or deer to eat. When the cheetah is close, he sprints after his prey.

Vocabulary:

cheetah: a big spotted cat that lives in Africa and is very fast
Africa: a continent that is south of Europe
slender: thin
prey: an animal that is killed and eaten by another animal
antelope: a deer-like animal that can run very fast

1 First Sentence: The cheetah, a large spotted cat from Africa, is the fastest animal in the world.

What did those words make you picture? _____

1. What did you see for the cheetah? _____

2. What did you picture for his spots? _____

3. What did you see for him being the fastest animal in the world? ____

4. What did you see for where he lives? _____

2 Second Sentence: With his long powerful legs and slender body, he can run up to 70 miles an hour.

What did those words make you picture? _____

1. What did you picture for his legs? _____

2. What did you picture for his body? _____

3. What did you see for him running 70 miles an hour? _____

4. Did you picture him running next to a car going 70, or did you picture the number 70, or both? _____

3 Third Sentence: But he can only run this fast for a short time.

What did those words make you picture? _____

_____

1. What did you see for how long he can run fast? _____

_____

2. How did you picture him running a short time really fast? _____

_____

3. What sounds did you hear? _____

_____

4. Were you picturing him running from up close or from far away? ____

4 Fourth Sentence: So the cheetah sneaks through the tall grass looking for a small antelope or deer to eat.

What did those words make you picture? _____

_____

1. What did you picture for the tall grass? _____

_____

2. What did you see for the cheetah sneaking in the grass? _____

_____

3. What did you picture for the deer? _____

_____

4. What sounds did you hear? _____

_____

5 Fifth Sentence: When the cheetah is close, he sprints after his prey.

What did those words make you picture? _____

_____

1. What did you picture for his prey—a deer, an antelope, or..? _____

_____

2. What did you see for the cheetah getting close to his prey? _____

_____

3. What did you see for him sprinting after his prey? _____

Picture Summary:

Number your images in order.

■   The cheetah sneaks through the tall grass looking for a small antelope.

■   The cheetah is the fastest animal in the world.

■   When the cheetah is close to the animals, he sprints after his prey.

■   With his long powerful legs, he can run up to 70 miles an hour for a short time.

Critical Thinking

Write a Word Summary:

_____

_____

_____

_____

_____

Main Idea:

Check the box that best describes all your images—the main idea.

- ☐ After quietly moving near an animal, the cheetah uses his great speed to catch his prey.

- ☐ With his long powerful legs and slender body, he can run up to 70 miles an hour.

- ☐ The cheetah, a large spotted cat from Africa, is the fastest animal in the world.

HOTS Questions:

1. Why do you think the cheetah is the fastest animal in the world? _____

2. Why do you think the cheetah needs powerful legs? _____

3. Why do you think he has a slender body? _____

4. What do you think would happen if he had a fat body and short legs? _____

5. Why do you think the cheetah sneaks through the grass looking for his prey? _____

6. Why do you think the cheetah waits until his prey is close before he runs after it? _____

Write a Story

Make up an exciting story about going on an adventure in Africa and seeing a cheetah.

_____
_____
_____
_____
_____
_____
_____
_____
_____
_____
_____
_____
_____
_____

Did you use all the Structure Words in your story? Check each one you used.

What	Size	Color	Mood	Background	Perspective
Number	Shape	Movement	Where	When	Sound

7 Mt. Rushmore

Gutzon Borglum and his team of workers carved giant faces on a mountain named Mt. Rushmore. He and his team used dynamite and air hammers to carve out the mountain. Tons of stone fell from the mountain as they worked to carve out the faces. Then 14 years later, the finished faces of Presidents Washington, Jefferson, Roosevelt, and Lincoln appeared. The faces are 60 feet tall and visited by more than 2 million people each year.

Sentence by Sentence
Date: _____

Vocabulary:

Mt. Rushmore: a mountain in South Dakota that has the faces of four Presidents carved on it
George Washington: the first president of the United States.
Thomas Jefferson: the third President of the U.S.
Theodore Roosevelt: the 26th President of the U.S.
Abraham Lincoln: the 16th President of the U.S.

---

1 First Sentence: Gutzon Borglum and his team of workers carved giant faces on a mountain named Mt. Rushmore.

What did those words make you picture? _____

1. What did you picture for Mt. Rushmore? _____

2. What did you see for Gutzon and his workers? _____

3. How did you see them carving the mountain? _____

4. How did you see them carving giant faces? _____

---

2 Second Sentence: He and his team used dynamite and air hammers to carve out the mountain.

What did those words make you picture? _____

1. What did you see for the dynamite? _____

2. What did you see for the air hammers? _____

3. What sounds did you hear? _____

4. What did you smell? _____

3 Third Sentence: Tons of stone fell from the mountain as they worked to carve out the faces.

What did those words make you picture? _____

_____

1. What did you see for tons of stone falling? _____

2. What did that sound like? _____

3. What did you see the workers doing? _____

4. Were you picturing this from up close or from far away? _____

4 Fourth Sentence: Then 14 years later, the finished faces of Presidents Washington, Jefferson, Roosevelt, and Lincoln appeared.

What did those words make you picture? _____

_____

1. What did you picture for 14 years later—did you picture a long time and the number? _____

2. What did you picture for the finished faces of the presidents? _____

3. Did you picture large faces or small faces? _____

4. How many presidents did you picture? _____

5 Fifth Sentence: The faces are 60 feet tall and visited by more than 2 million people each year.

What did those words make you picture? _____

_____

1. What did you picture for the size of the faces? _____

2. What did you see for people visiting Mt. Rushmore? _____

3. How many people did you see visiting over a whole year? _____

Picture Summary:

Number your images in order.

▪ Gutzon Borglum and his team used dynamite and air hammers to carve out the mountain.

▪ The faces are 60 feet tall and visited by more than 2 million people each year.

▪ Tons of stone fell from the mountain as they worked to carve the faces.

▪ Then 14 years later, the finished faces of Presidents Washington, Jefferson, Roosevelt, and Lincoln appeared.

Critical Thinking

Write a Word Summary:

_____

_____

_____

_____

Main Idea:

Check the box that best describes all your images—the main idea.

☐ Gutzon Borglum and his team used dynamite and air hammers to carve a mountain.

☐ The faces of Washington, Jefferson, Roosevelt, and Lincoln are 60 feet high.

☐ Gutzon Borglum and his team worked for years to carve the faces of four presidents on Mt. Rushmore.

HOTS Questions:

1. Why do you think Gutzon needed a team of workers to carve Mt. Rushmore? _____

2. Why do you think they used dynamite instead of small hand tools to carve out the mountain? _____

3. Why do you think they used large air hammers instead of regular hammers? _____

4. Why do you think it took 14 years to carve out the mountain? _____

5. Why do you think they carved a mountain instead of making a small statue? _____

6. Why do you think Gutzon only carved four presidents and not more? _____

Write a Story

Make up a story about the dangers of creating the faces of Mt. Rushmore.

_____
_____
_____
_____
_____
_____
_____
_____
_____
_____
_____
_____
_____
_____
_____

Did you use all the Structure Words in your story? Check each one you used.

What	Size	Color	Mood	Background	Perspective
Number	Shape	Movement	Where	When	Sound

8 A Life After Death

Sentence by Sentence
Date: _____

Pharaohs in ancient Egypt spent a lot of time getting their things packed and ready for their death. They thought that death led to a new life, and they wanted to have things that they had before they died. They built big tombs with many rooms that they filled with the things they would need in the next world. They packed treasures, tools and household goods, clothes, and chariots. The better they packed their tomb, the more stuff they would have in the next life.

Vocabulary:

pharaohs: the rulers of ancient Egypt;
ancient: a long time ago
Egypt: a country in North Africa
tomb: the place where a dead person is buried
chariot: a cart with two wheels that is pulled by horses

---

1 First Sentence: Pharaohs in ancient Egypt spent a lot of time getting their things packed and ready for their death.

What did those words make you picture? _____

_____

1. What did you picture for a pharaoh? _____

2. What did you see for ancient Egypt? _____

3. What did you see for their things? _____

4. What did you see for the pharaohs "packing?" _____

---

2 Second Sentence: They thought that death led to a new life, and they wanted to have things that they had before they died.

What did those words make you picture? _____

_____

1. What did you see for "death led to a new life?" _____

2. What did you see for a new life? _____

3. What did you see for some of the things that they had before they died? _____

4. What did you see for their mood about dying? _____

3 Third Sentence: They built big tombs with many rooms that they filled with the things they would need in the next world.

What did those words make you picture? _____

_____

1. What did you see for big tombs? _____

_____

2. What did you see for what the big tombs were made of? _____

_____

3. What did you see for the many rooms in the tomb? _____

_____

4. What did you picture a room would look like? _____

4 Fourth Sentence: They packed treasures, tools and household goods, clothes, and chariots.

What did those words make you picture? _____

_____

1. What did you see for them packing their treasures? _____

_____

2. What did you picture for their tools? _____

_____

3. What did you picture for their household goods? _____

_____

4. What did you picture for the chariots? _____

5 Fifth Sentence: The better they packed their tomb, the more stuff they would have in the next life.

What did those words make you picture? _____

_____

1. What did you picture for their stuff? _____

_____

2. What did you picture for how much they would have in the next life? _____

_____

3. Did you picture the tombs packed with lots of stuff or a little? _____

Picture Summary:

Number your images in order.

▢ Pharaohs packed treasures, tools and household goods, clothes, and chariots.

▢ Pharaohs in ancient Egypt spent a lot of time getting their things packed for their death.

▢ Pharaohs thought that death led to a new life, and they wanted to have things that they had before they died.

▢ Pharaohs built big tombs with many rooms that they filled with the things they would need in the next world.

Critical Thinking

Write a Word Summary:

_____

_____

_____

_____

Main Idea:

Check the box that best describes all your images—the main idea.

☐ The pharaohs built big tombs with many rooms.

☐ The pharaohs thought that death led to a new life.

☐ The pharaohs built big tombs and filled them with things they might need in the next life.

HOTS Questions:

1. Why do you think pharaohs spent a lot of time getting their things packed for death? _____

2. Why do you think they wanted to bring things with them? _____

3. Why do you think they thought that death brought a new life? _____

4. Why do you think they wanted games? _____

5. Why do you think they built big tombs? _____

6. Why do you think their tombs needed many rooms? _____

Write a Story

Make up a story about discovering an Egyptian tomb.

_____
_____
_____
_____
_____
_____
_____
_____
_____
_____
_____
_____
_____
_____
_____

Did you use all the Structure Words in your story? Check each one you used.

What	Size	Color	Mood	Background	Perspective
Number	Shape	Movement	Where	When	Sound

9 The PB & J

One of the best sandwiches of all time is the peanut butter and jelly sandwich. It was first made by army troops, in camps during World War II. Their rations came with cans of peanut butter and grape jelly, and white bread. The soldiers mixed them to get a snack they could eat on the run. They brought the easy and tasty sandwich idea home after the war.

Vocabulary:

World War II: a war that was fought from 1939 to 1945 by many countries
army troops: a group of people in the army
rations: the food given to a soldier

Sentence by Sentence
Date: _____

1 First Sentence: One of the best sandwiches of all time is the peanut butter and jelly sandwich.

What did those words make you picture? _____

1. What did you picture for a sandwich? _____

2. What did you picture for peanut butter? _____

3. What did you picture for jelly? _____

4. Could you picture the taste and smell of the sandwich? _____

2 Second Sentence: It was first made by army troops, in camps during World War II.

What did those words make you picture? _____

1. What did you see for army troops? _____

2. What did you see for the troops making the sandwich? _____

3. What did you see for their camp? _____

4. What sounds did you hear? _____

3 Third Sentence: Their rations came with cans of peanut butter and grape jelly, and white bread.

What did those words make you picture? _____

1. What did you picture for rations? _____

2. What did you picture for a can of peanut butter? _____

3. What did you picture for grape jelly? _____

4. What color and size did you see the bread? _____

4 Fourth Sentence: The soldiers mixed them to get a snack they could eat on the run.

What did those words make you picture? _____

1. What did you see for the soldiers? _____

2. What did you picture for the soldiers' clothes? _____

3. How did you see them mixing peanut butter and jelly? _____

4. What did you picture for eating on the run? _____

5 Fifth Sentence: They brought the easy and tasty sandwich idea home after the war.

What did those words make you picture? _____

1. What did you see for the sandwich being easy and tasty? _____

2. What did you see for the soldiers bringing the sandwich idea home? _____

3. What did you see for their home? _____

Picture Summary:

Number your images in order.

☐ Soldiers' rations came with cans of peanut butter and grape jelly, and white bread.

☐ They brought the easy and tasty sandwich idea home after the war.

☐ The soldiers mixed them to get a snack they could eat on the run.

☐ One of the best sandwiches of all time was first made by army troops, in camps during World War II.

Critical Thinking

Write a Word Summary:

_____
_____
_____
_____
_____

Main Idea:

Check the box that best describes all your images—the main idea.

☐ Soldiers brought peanut butter and jelly sandwiches home after the war.

☐ Army rations came with peanut butter and grape jelly.

☐ Soldiers in World War II created the peanut butter and jelly sandwich.

HOTS Questions:

1. Why do you think the peanut butter and jelly sandwich is considered one of the best sandwiches? _____
_____

2. Why do you think soldiers got their food in cans? _____
_____

3. How do you think they would eat the jelly and peanut butter if they didn't make a sandwich? _____
_____

4. Why do you think the army troops mixed up peanut butter and jelly and bread? _____
_____

5. Why do you think they needed something they could eat on the run? _____
_____

6. Why do you think the peanut butter and jelly sandwich became popular at home too? _____
_____

Write a Story

Make up a funny story about eating a peanut butter and jelly sandwich.

Did you use all the Structure Words in your story? Check each one you used.

What	Size	Color	Mood	Background	Perspective
Number	Shape	Movement	Where	When	Sound

10 Ice Festival

People in Harbin, China, brave the bitter winter cold for their annual ice festival. Huge blocks of ice are cut from the frozen river. The ice is brought to the park and carved into statues of warriors and great temples. Bright lights inside the ice shine as people walk by them. When the festival is over, these works of art are smashed.

Sentence by Sentence
Date: _____

Vocabulary:

China: a large country in Asia
bitter cold: very, very cold
annual: something that happens every year
festival: celebration; a special event

---

1 **First Sentence:** People in Harbin, China, brave the bitter winter cold for their annual ice festival.

What did those words make you picture? _____

1. What did you picture for China? _____

2. What did you picture for winter? _____

3. How did you see the people dressed? _____

4. What did you see for an annual festival? _____

---

2 **Second Sentence:** Huge blocks of ice are cut from the frozen river.

What did those words make you picture? _____

1. What did you picture for the blocks of ice? _____

2. What did you picture for the size of the blocks? _____

3. How did you see the frozen river? _____

4. How did you see the ice being cut from the river? _____

3 **Third Sentence:** The ice is brought to the park and carved into statues of warriors and great temples.

What did those words make you picture? _____
_____
_____

1. How did you picture the ice being brought to the park? _____
_____

2. How did you see it being carved? _____
_____

3. What did you see for the statues? _____
_____

4. What size did you picture the ice statues? _____
_____

4 **Fourth Sentence:** Bright lights inside the ice shine as people walk by them.

What did those words make you picture? _____
_____
_____

1. What did you see for the bright lights inside the ice? _____
_____

2. What did you picture for the ice shining? _____
_____

3. How did you see the people walking by the ice? _____
_____

4. What sounds did you hear? _____
_____

5 **Fifth Sentence:** When the festival is over, these works of art are smashed.

What did those words make you picture? _____
_____

1. What did you picture for the festival being over? _____
_____

2. What did you picture for the art being smashed? _____
_____

3. What sounds did you hear? _____
_____

Picture Summary:

Number your images in order.

☐ The ice is carved into statues of warriors and great temples.

☐ Huge blocks of ice are cut from the frozen river and brought to the park.

☐ When the festival is over, the icy works of art are smashed.

☐ People in Harbin, China, have an annual ice festival.

Critical Thinking

Write a Word Summary:

_____
_____
_____
_____

Main Idea:

Check the box that best describes all your images—the main idea.

☐ Huge blocks of ice are cut from the frozen river during Harbin's annual ice festival.

☐ Bright lights shine inside temples made of ice as people walk by them.

☐ Beautiful ice sculptures line the park in Harbin, China, during the annual ice festival.

HOTS Questions:

1. Why do you think the people in Harbin go to the festival in the bitter cold winter? _____

2. Why do you think this festival is held in the winter and not in the spring? _____

3. Why do you think they cut blocks of ice from a frozen river instead of making it themselves? _____

4. Why do you think the ice is carved in a park and not inside a building? _____

5. Why do you think they put lights inside the ice? _____

6. Why do you think these works of art are smashed at the end of the festival? _____

Write a Story

Make up a story about anything you want!

Did you use all the Structure Words in your story? Check each one you used.

What	Size	Color	Mood	Background	Perspective
Number	Shape	Movement	Where	When	Sound

11 Purple Legs

Although wine is no longer made by people crushing grapes with their feet, some still do it for fun. During the fall, some wineries invite people to come and stomp grapes. Tourists of all ages gladly take off their shoes and wash their feet before stepping into a big vat of purple grapes. Then they walk, dance, and run around the vat. When they climb out, their feet and legs are purple from the grape juice.

Vocabulary:

wine: a drink that is made from grapes
wineries: places where wine is made from grapes
tourists: travelers; someone who travels for fun
vat: a large round tub

---

1 First Sentence: Although wine is no longer made by people crushing grapes with their feet, some still do it for fun.

What did those words make you picture? _____

_____

1. What did you see for wine? _____

2. What did you picture for grapes? _____

3. How did you see people crushing grapes? _____

4. What did you see for their feet? _____

2 Second Sentence: During the fall, some wineries invite people to come and stomp grapes.

What did those words make you picture? _____

_____

1. What did you picture for the fall? _____

2. What did you see for a winery? _____

3. What did you see for people coming to the winery? _____

4. What did you see for "stomping" grapes? _____

3. Third Sentence: Tourists of all ages gladly take off their shoes and wash their feet before stepping into a big vat of purple grapes.

What did those words make you picture? _____

_____

1. What did you see for the tourists? _____

2. What did you picture for them taking off their shoes? _____

3. How did you see them washing their feet? _____

4. What did you picture for the big vat of grapes? _____

4. Fourth Sentence: Then they walk, dance, and run around the vat.

What did those words make you picture? _____

_____

1. What did you see for them walking in the vat? _____

2. How did you see them dancing in the vat? _____

3. What did you hear? _____

4. What did you picture happening to the grapes? _____

5. Fifth Sentence: When they climb out, their feet and legs are purple from the grape juice.

What did those words make you picture? _____

_____

1. What did you see for the people climbing out? _____

2. What did you picture for their feet now? _____

3. What did you see for the grapes in the vat now? _____

Picture Summary:

Number your images in order.

▇ People take off their shoes and wash their feet before stepping into a big vat of purple grapes.

▇ During the fall, some wineries invite people to come and stomp grapes.

▇ When the people climb out of the vat, their feet and legs are purple from the grape juice.

▇ The people walk, dance, and run around the vat.

Critical Thinking

Write a Word Summary:

_____

_____

_____

_____

Main Idea:

Check the box that best describes all your images—the main idea.

☐ Tourists take off their shoes and step into a big vat of grapes.

☐ When the tourists climb out of the vat, their feet and legs are purple.

☐ During the fall, tourists visit wineries and stomp grapes.

HOTS Questions:

1. Why do you think wine is no longer made by people crushing the grapes with their feet? _____

2. Why do you think some people stomp grapes for fun? _____

3. Why do you think they take off their shoes before they stomp? _____

4. Why do you think they wash their feet first? _____

5. Why do you think they dance and run around the vat? _____

6. Why do you think their legs are also purple and not just their feet? _____

Write a Story

Make up a funny story about stomping grapes!

_____

Did you use all the Structure Words in your story? Check each one you used.

What	Size	Color	Mood	Background	Perspective
Number	Shape	Movement	Where	When	Sound

12 The Giants of the Forest

Each day, thousands of people go to the redwood forest to look at the giant trees. The tallest redwood stands higher than the Statue of Liberty. Other huge redwood trees grow around it and help protect it from the wind. Because these trees grow close together, they block much of the sunlight. People walk in the dark woods and feel like kids in a world of giants.

Sentence by Sentence
Date: _____

Vocabulary:

redwood forest: a forest where most of the trees are giant redwoods
Statue of Liberty: a huge statue that is 305 tall and stands in the middle of New York Harbor

---

1 **First Sentence:** Each day, thousands of people go to the redwood forest to look at the giant trees.

What did those words make you picture? _____

1. What did you see for the redwood forest? _____

2. What did you see for the giant trees? _____

3. What size did you picture for the trunk of the tree? _____

4. How did you see people visiting the forest? _____

---

2 **Second Sentence:** The tallest redwood stands higher than the Statue of Liberty.

What did those words make you picture? _____

1. What did you see for the tallest redwood? _____

2. What color did you picture the trunk? _____

3. What did you see for the Statue of Liberty? _____

4. Did you picture the tallest redwood tree being taller or shorter than the Statue of Liberty?

3. Third Sentence: Other huge redwood trees grow around it and help protect it from the wind.

What did those words make you picture? _____
_____
_____

1. What did you see for the other redwoods growing around the tallest tree? _____

2. What did you see for the size of those trees? _____
_____

3. What sounds did you hear? _____
_____

4. Were you picturing this up close or from far away? _____

4. Fourth Sentence: Because these trees grow close together, they block much of the sunlight.

What did those words make you picture? _____
_____
_____

1. What did you see for the trees growing close together? _____
_____

2. How much space did you see between the trees? _____
_____

3. What color did you picture for the forest? _____
_____

4. What did you see for sunlight blocked out? _____
_____

5. Fifth Sentence: People walk in the dark woods and feel like kids in a world of giants.

What did those words make you picture? _____
_____
_____

1. What did you see for people walking? _____
_____

2. What did you see for it being dark? _____
_____

3. What did you see for the people feeling like they are in a world of giants? _____

Picture Summary:

Number your images in order.

☐ The tallest redwood stands higher than the Statue of Liberty.

☐ Each day, thousands of people go to the redwood forest to look at the giant trees.

☐ People walk in the dark woods and feel like kids in a world of giants.

☐ Other huge redwoods grow close to each other, blocking much of the sunlight.

Critical Thinking

Write a Word Summary:

_____
_____
_____
_____

Main Idea:

Check the box that best describes all your images—the main idea.

☐ The people who walk in the redwood forest feel like kids in a world of giants.

☐ The tallest tree in the redwood forest is taller than the Statue of Liberty.

☐ The trees of the redwood forest are the tallest in the world and a popular place for visitors.

HOTS Questions:

1. Why do you think so many people want to see the redwood trees? _____
_____

2. How do you think having other huge redwoods around might protect the tallest redwood? _____
_____

3. Why do you think this forest is dark? _____
_____

4. How do you think these trees block out the sunlight? _____
_____

5. Why do you think the people who visit feel like kids? _____
_____

6. How do you think you would feel standing next to these trees? _____
_____

Write a Story

Make up a scary story about getting lost in a redwood forest.

_____
_____
_____
_____
_____
_____
_____
_____
_____
_____
_____
_____
_____
_____

Did you use all the Structure Words in your story? Check each one you used.

What	Size	Color	Mood	Background	Perspective
Number	Shape	Movement	Where	When	Sound

13 Race to the Top

Once a year, there is a race up the stairs of the Empire State Building. Over 100 people run up the 1,576 steps to the top. Because so many people compete, everyone can't be at the starting line at the same time. The runners wear a computer chip that marks when they start and finish. The person with the fastest time, often less than ten minutes, wins.

Sentence by Sentence
Date: _____

Vocabulary:

Empire State Building: a very tall building in New York City
compete: to be in a race or contest

---

1 First Sentence: Once a year, there is a race up the stairs of the Empire State Building.

What did those words make you picture? _____

_____

_____

1. What did you see for the Empire State Building? _____

_____

2. How tall did you see the building? _____

_____

3. What did you see for a race up the stairs? _____

_____

4. What sounds did you hear? _____

---

2 Second Sentence: Over 100 people run up the 1,576 steps to the top.

What did those words make you picture? _____

_____

_____

1. What did you see for the steps? _____

_____

2. How did you picture the 1,576 steps? _____

_____

3. What did you see for over 100 people running up the stairs? _____

_____

4. What did you see for the top of the building? _____

3. Third Sentence: Because so many people compete, everyone can't be at the starting line at the same time.

What did those words make you picture? _____
_____

1. What did you see for the runners competing in the race? _____
   _____

2. How were they dressed? _____
   _____

3. What did you see for the first one to finish but not win? _____
   _____

4. What mood did you picture for that person?! _____
   _____

4. Fourth Sentence: The runners wear a computer chip that marks when they start and finish.

What did those words make you picture? _____
_____

1. What did you see for a computer chip? _____
   _____

2. What did you see for the runners wearing the chip? _____
   _____

3. Where did you see the runners putting the chip on their bodies? _____
   _____

4. What did you hear for the computer chip marking the start and finish?
   _____

5. Fifth Sentence: The person with the fastest time, often less than ten minutes, wins.

What did those words make you picture? _____
_____

1. What did you see for the runner with the fastest time? _____
   _____

2. How fast did you see that runner going up the steps? _____
   _____

3. What did you see for the mood of the winner? _____
   _____

Picture Summary:

Number your images in order.

[ ] Once a year, there is a race up the stairs of the Empire State Building.

[ ] The person with the fastest time wins.

[ ] The runners wear a computer chip that marks when they start and finish the race.

[ ] Over 100 people run up the 1,576 steps to the top.

Critical Thinking

Write a Word Summary:

_____

_____

_____

_____

Main Idea:

Check the box that best describes all your images—the main idea.

☐ Over 100 people run up the 1,576 steps to the top of the Empire State Building.

☐ The runners wear a computer chip that marks when they start and finish the race.

☐ Once a year, runners race to the top of the Empire State Building.

HOTS Questions:

1. Why do you think people might want to race to the top of the Empire State Building? _____

2. How is this race different than most races? _____

3. Do you think that normal runners can easily win in this race? Why or why not? _____

4. What about the height of the Empire State Building makes it a difficult race? _____

5. Do you think 100 people racing up the stairs might be a problem? Why? _____

6. What might be a reason that the first person to finish might not be the winner? _____

Write a Story

Make up an exciting story about a race.

Did you use all the Structure Words in your story? Check each one you used.

What	Size	Color	Mood	Background	Perspective
Number	Shape	Movement	Where	When	Sound

14 Sliding Ride

Sentence by Sentence
Date: _____

Sleds have carried people and supplies in cold snowy weather for hundreds of years. Usually made of wood or metal, they sit on flat runners, not wheels. This means they can slide easily across ice and snow. Sleds are used for work and for fun because they can carry people or goods. Strong horses, dogs, or reindeer can be harnessed to the sleds to pull them.

Vocabulary:

sled: a small or large cart or platform that is on long flat blades and is pulled across the snow by animals or to slide down hills
supplies: food and other important items
runners: long thin blades on the bottom of a sled
harness: a set of straps that an animal wears so that it can pull a sled

---

1 First Sentence: Sleds have carried people and supplies in cold snowy weather for hundreds of years.

What did those words make you picture? _____
_____
_____

1. What did you see for a sled? _____
_____

2. What did you see for the people in a sled? _____
_____

3. What did you see for their supplies? _____
_____

4. What did you see for where sleds are used? _____
_____

---

2 Second Sentence: Usually made of wood or metal, they sit on flat runners, not wheels.

What did those words make you picture? _____
_____
_____

1. What did you picture for what a sled is made of? _____
_____

2. What did you picture for flat runners? _____
_____

3. Did you picture the runners as made of metal or wood? _____
_____

4. What did you see about runners that is different than wheels? ___
_____

3 Third Sentence: This means they can slide easily across ice and snow.

What did those words make you picture? _____
_____
_____

1. What did you picture for a sled sliding easily? _____
_____

2. What did you picture for where the sled slides? _____
_____

3. What did you picture for snow? _____
_____

4. What did you picture for the sound of a sled sliding across ice or snow?
_____

4 Fourth Sentence: Sleds are used for work and for fun because they can carry people or goods.

What did those words make you picture? _____
_____
_____

1. What did you picture for a sled being used for work? _____
_____

2. What did you picture for it carrying goods? _____
_____

3. What did you picture for a sled being used for fun? _____
_____

4. What sounds did you hear for fun? _____
_____

5 Fifth Sentence: Strong horses, dogs, or reindeer can be harnessed to the sleds to pull them.

What did those words make you picture? _____
_____
_____

1. What did you see for strong horses? _____
_____

2. What did you see for horses being harnessed to a sled? _____
_____

3. What did you picture for reindeer pulling a sled? _____
_____

Picture Summary:

Number your images in order.

■ Sleds are used for work and for fun.

■ Sleds have carried people and supplies in cold snowy weather for years.

■ Sleds are made of metal or wood and have flat runners, not wheels.

■ Strong horses, dogs, or reindeer are harnessed to the sleds to pull them.

Critical Thinking

Write a Word Summary:

_____

_____

_____

_____

_____

_____

Main Idea:

Check the box that best describes all your images—the main idea.

☐ Sleds don't have wheels.

☐ Sleds are made of wood or metal and sit on flat runners.

☐ Sleds carry people and goods in snowy weather.

HOTS Questions:

1. Why do you think people use sleds and not cars in the snow? _____

2. Why do you think sleds are made of wood or metal and not cloth? _____

3. Why do you think sleds sit on flat runners? _____

4. Why do you think it is important for a sled to be able to slide across ice? _____

5. Why do you think sleds could carry either people or goods? _____

6. Why do you think strong animals are used to pull sleds? _____

Write a Story

Make up a story about a winter adventure on a sled.

_____

Did you use all the Structure Words in your story? Check each one you used.

What	Size	Color	Mood	Background	Perspective
Number	Shape	Movement	Where	When	Sound

15 Nessie

There may be a sea monster in a huge lake called Loch Ness in Scotland. For years, the monster, named Nessie, has been seen by people fishing or camping at the lake. They say she has a long neck that lifts her head far out of the water. Some think that Nessie is a living dinosaur, but no one has been able to prove if she exists.

Sentence by Sentence
Date: _____

Vocabulary:

loch: a large lake in Scotland
Scotland: a country in Europe that is part of Great Britain
dinosaur: an animal that lived millions of years ago

---

1 First Sentence: There may be a sea monster in a huge lake called Loch Ness in Scotland.

What did those words make you picture? _____
_____
_____

1. What did you picture for a sea monster? _____
   _____

2. What did you see for Loch Ness? _____
   _____

3. What did you picture for the size of the lake? _____
   _____

4. How did you picture Scotland? _____
   _____

---

2 Second Sentence: For years, the monster, named Nessie, has been seen by people fishing or camping at the lake.

What did those words make you picture? _____
_____
_____

1. What did you see for Nessie? _____
   _____

2. How did you picture people fishing? _____
   _____

3. What mood did you see for the people who saw Nessie? _____
   _____

4. How did you see people camping? _____
   _____

3 **Third Sentence:** They say she has a long neck that lifts her head far out of the water.

What did those words make you picture? _____

_____

1. What did you picture for her neck? _____

2. What did you picture for her head? _____

3. What did you see her doing with her head? _____

4. What did you see for the size of her head and neck? _____

4 **Fourth Sentence:** Some think that Nessie is a living dinosaur, but no one has been able to prove if she exists.

What did those words make you picture? _____

_____

1. What did you see for a dinosaur? _____

2. What did you picture for Nessie now? _____

3. Were you picturing her from up close or from far away? _____

4. What did you see for no one being able to prove that she exists? _____

Picture Summary:

Number your images in order.

☐ For years, a monster named Nessie has been seen by people fishing or camping at the lake.

☐ Nessie may be a living dinosaur, but no one has been able to prove if she exists.

☐ They say Nessie has a long neck that lifts her head far out of the water.

☐ There may be a sea monster named Nessie in a huge lake called Loch Ness in Scotland.

Write a Word Summary:

_____

_____

_____

_____

_____

_____

_____

Critical Thinking

Main Idea:

Check the box that best describes all your images—the main idea.

☐ A sea monster named Nessie may live in Loch Ness in Scotland.

☐ Some people think Nessie is a living dinosaur.

☐ Nessie has a long neck that lifts her head far out of the water.

HOTS Questions:

1. Why do you think people believe a sea monster might live in Loch Ness? _____

2. Why do you think people might choose to go camping at Loch Ness? _____

3. Why do you think Nessie lifts her head out of the water? _____

4. Why do you think some people believe she is a dinosaur? _____

5. Why do you think the story says a "living" dinosaur? _____

6. Why do you think no one has proven Nessie's existence? _____

7. Do you think Nessie exists? Why or why not? _____

Write a Story

Make up a story about what happened one day fishing and seeing Nessie!

_____

Did you use all the Structure Words in your story? Check each one you used.

What	Size	Color	Mood	Background	Perspective
Number	Shape	Movement	Where	When	Sound

16 Kellogg Invents Cereal

In 1894, Will Kellogg tried to make wheat crackers, but instead made the first flaked cereal. Will set aside a pot of boiled wheat to be made into crackers. After the wheat had cooled, he tried to roll it into long thin sheets to cut into crackers. But the wheat dough broke into small flakes. Will decided to bake the flakes and then he served them with milk as a crunchy breakfast cereal.

Sentence by Sentence
Date: _____

Vocabulary:

sheets: long thin flat pieces
dough: a mix of flour, water, and other things
flakes: small thin pieces

1

First Sentence: In 1894, Will Kellogg tried to make wheat crackers, but instead made the first flaked cereal.

What did those words make you picture? _____

1. What did you see for Will Kellogg? _____

2. What did you see for wheat crackers? _____

3. What did you see him doing? _____

4. What did you picture for the cereal? _____

2

Second Sentence: Will set aside a pot of boiled wheat to be made into crackers.

What did those words make you picture? _____

1. What did you see Will doing now? _____

2. What size pot did you picture? _____

3. What color did you picture for the wheat? _____

4. How did you see the wheat in the pot? _____

3. Third Sentence: After the wheat had cooled, he tried to roll it into long thin sheets to cut into crackers.

What did those words make you picture? _____
_____
_____

1. What did you see for rolling the wheat? _____
   _____

2. What did you picture for crackers? _____
   _____

3. Where did you see Will rolling the wheat? _____
   _____

4. How did you see long thin sheets? _____
   _____

4. Fourth Sentence: But the wheat dough broke into small flakes.

What did those words make you picture? _____
_____
_____

1. What did you see for small flakes? _____
   _____

2. What color did you picture the flakes? _____
   _____

3. What did you picture for Will's mood when the wheat broke into small flakes?
   _____

4. What did you picture Will doing with the wheat flakes? _____
   _____

5. Fifth Sentence: Will decided to bake the flakes and then he served them with milk as a crunchy breakfast cereal.

What did those words make you picture? _____
_____

1. What did you see for baking the flakes? _____
   _____

2. What did you picture Will serving the flakes in? _____
   _____

3. What did you picture Will pouring over the cereal? _____
   _____

Picture Summary:

Number your images in order.

☐ Will served the flakes with milk.

☐ The wheat dough broke into small flakes.

☐ Will set aside a pot of boiled wheat to make crackers.

☐ Will tried to roll the wheat into long thin sheets.

Critical Thinking

Write a Word Summary:

_____
_____
_____
_____

Main Idea:

Check the box that best describes all your images—the main idea.

- [ ] Will decided to bake the flakes and then served them with milk as a breakfast cereal.

- [ ] Will Kellogg tried to make crackers but made the first flaked breakfast cereal instead.

- [ ] The wheat dough broke into small flakes.

HOTS Questions:

1. Why do you think Will set aside the pot of wheat after he boiled it? _____

2. Why do you think he tried to roll the wheat into thin sheets? _____

3. Why do you think crackers need to be made from long thin sheets of dough? _____

4. Why do you think the wheat broke into flakes? _____

5. Why do you think Will served the flakes with milk? _____

6. What do you think the reaction to the new food was? _____

Write a Story

Make up a story about anything you want!

_____
_____
_____
_____
_____
_____
_____
_____
_____
_____
_____
_____
_____
_____

Did you use all the Structure Words in your story? Check each one you used.

What	Size	Color	Mood	Background	Perspective
Number	Shape	Movement	Where	When	Sound

17 One Small Step

The white space capsule landed gently on the dusty surface of the moon. The astronaut, Neil Armstrong, held his breath as he began to climb down the ladder. He jumped off the last step and landed on the powdery surface of the moon. With one small step, Armstrong became the first man to walk on the moon.

Sentence by Sentence
Date: _____

Vocabulary:

capsule: a small space ship
surface: the outer or top part
astronaut: a person trained to travel and work in space
powdery: soft and dry

---

1 First Sentence: The white space capsule landed gently on the dusty surface of the moon.

What did those words make you picture? _____

_____

_____

1. What did you see for the space capsule? _____

_____

2. What color did you picture the capsule? _____

_____

3. Did you picture the capsule landing gently or crashing on the moon?

_____

4. What did you picture for the moon's surface? _____

_____

---

2 Second Sentence: The astronaut, Neil Armstrong, held his breath as he began to climb down the ladder.

What did those words make you picture? _____

_____

_____

1. What did you see for the astronaut? _____

_____

2. What did you see the astronaut doing? _____

_____

3. Did you picture the astronaut climbing down the ladder quickly or slowly?

_____

4. How did you see him holding his breath? _____

_____

3. Third Sentence: He jumped off the last step and landed on the powdery surface of the moon.

What did those words make you picture? _____

1. Did you picture him making a big jump or a little hop? _____

2. What did you picture for the ground? _____

3. What did you picture for powdery? _____

4. What did you picture for the mood of the astronaut? _____

4. Fourth Sentence: With one small step, Armstrong became the first man to walk on the moon.

What did those words make you picture? _____

1. What did you see for "one small step?" _____

2. How did you picture Armstrong walking on the moon—slow or fast? _____

3. How many people did you picture walking on the moon the first time? _____

4. How many people did you see walking on the moon before Armstrong? _____

Picture Summary:

Number your images in order.

▮ Armstrong was the first to walk on the moon.

▮ Armstrong jumped off the ladder.

▮ Armstrong climbed down the ladder.

▮ Armstrong held his breath.

Write a Word Summary:

_____
_____
_____
_____
_____
_____
_____

Critical Thinking

Write a Word Summary:

_____

_____

_____

_____

Main Idea:

Check the box that best describes all your images—the main idea.

☐ Neil Armstrong held his breath as he climbed down the ladder.

☐ The white space capsule landed gently on the dusty surface of the moon.

☐ With one step, Neil Armstrong became the first man to walk on the moon.

HOTS Questions:

1. Why do you think Armstrong had to use a space capsule to get to the moon? _____

2. Why do you think Armstrong held his breath when he reached the last step of the ladder? _____

3. Why do you think he might have looked down before he jumped? _____

4. Why do you think no one had walked on the moon before Armstrong? _____

5. Why do you think Armstrong's first step was so important? _____

6. What do you think happened next? _____

Write a Story

Make up a story about taking a trip to the moon.

_____
_____
_____
_____
_____
_____
_____
_____
_____
_____
_____
_____
_____
_____

Did you use all the Structure Words in your story? Check each one you used.

What	Size	Color	Mood	Background	Perspective
Number	Shape	Movement	Where	When	Sound

18 Kasparov and Deep Blue

In 1996, Gary Kasparov, the world chess champion, sat down to a chess match against a computer. He sat in front of a real chess set while the computer, Deep Blue, told which pieces it wanted to move. In the first game, the computer won in less than three hours. That night Gary studied all the moves Deep Blue had made. Then he came back the next day and won three games and the match.

Vocabulary:

chess: a board game that is played by two people
chess match: a series of chess games where the person who wins the most games wins the match
computer: a machine that is used to store and figure out information

---

1 First Sentence: In 1996, Gary Kasparov, the world chess champion, sat down to a chess match against a computer.

What did those words make you picture? _____

_____

1. What did you picture for Gary? _____

2. Where did you see him sitting? _____

3. What did you picture sitting across from Gary? _____

4. What did you see for the computer? _____

---

2 Second Sentence: He sat in front of a real chess set while the computer, Deep Blue, told which pieces it wanted to move.

What did those words make you picture? _____

_____

1. What did you see for the chess set in front of Gary? _____

2. What colors did you picture for the chess set? _____

3. What did you picture for the chess pieces? _____

4. How did you see the computer telling the pieces to move? _____

3. Third Sentence: In the first game, the computer won in less than three hours.

What did those words make you picture? _____

_____

1. What did you see happening in the first game? _____

2. What did it look like when the computer was winning? _____

3. What mood did you picture for Gary? _____

4. Were you picturing all this from up close or from far away? _____

4. Fourth Sentence: That night Gary studied all the moves Deep Blue had made.

What did those words make you picture? _____

_____

1. What did you picture Gary doing now? _____

2. Where did you picture him studying? _____

3. How did you see him studying Deep Blue's moves? _____

4. How did you picture it being night? _____

5. Fifth Sentence: Then he came back the next day and won three games and the match.

What did those words make you picture? _____

_____

1. What did you see for Gary coming back? _____

2. What did you see for his mood when he started? _____

3. What did you see for him winning three games? _____

Picture Summary:

Number your images in order.

☐ In the first game, the computer won in less than three hours.

☐ Then he came back and won three games and the match.

☐ In 1996, Gary Kasparov, the world chess champion, played a chess match against a computer.

☐ That night, Gary studied all the moves Deep Blue had made.

Critical Thinking

Write a Word Summary:

_____

_____

_____

_____

Main Idea:

Check the box that best describes all your images—the main idea.

☐ In 1996, Gary Kasparov beat a computer in a chess match.

☐ A computer, named Deep Blue, beat Kasparov in the first game.

☐ Gary Kasparov studied all the moves Deep Blue had made.

HOTS Questions:

1. Why do you think Gary might want to play chess against a computer? _____

2. Do you think Gary was confident in his skill if he was willing to play a computer? Explain. _____

3. How do you think the computer knew which pieces to move? _____

4. What might be a reason why the computer won the first game so quickly? _____

5. Why do you think Gary studied all the moves the computer made in the first game? _____

6. Why do you think Gary was able to win the match? _____

Write a Story

Make up a story about anything you want!

_____
_____
_____
_____
_____
_____
_____
_____
_____
_____
_____
_____
_____
_____

Did you use all the Structure Words in your story? Check each one you used.

What □	Size □	Color □	Mood □	Background □	Perspective □
Number □	Shape □	Movement □	Where □	When □	Sound □

19 A Bug in the Computer

In 1947, Grace Hopper was designing computers at Harvard University. The computer was not working right, so Grace looked inside. She reached in with a pair of tweezers and pulled out a moth. Then the computer started to work fine. Since that time, when a problem on a computer is fixed, it is said to be "debugged."

Vocabulary:

designing: planning and building
university: a school of higher learning
tweezers: a long thin tool that is used to pick up small objects
moth: a flying insect that is like a butterfly

---

1 First Sentence: In 1947, Grace Hopper was designing computers at Harvard University.

What did those words make you picture? _____

_____

_____

1. What did you see for Grace? _____

_____

2. What did you see her doing? _____

_____

3. Where did you see her using the computer? _____

_____

4. What did you see for the date? _____

---

2 Second Sentence: The computer was not working right, so Grace looked inside.

What did those words make you picture? _____

_____

_____

1. What did you see for the computer not working right? _____

_____

2. What did you picture for Grace's mood? _____

_____

3. What did you see her doing to look inside? _____

_____

4. What did you see for inside the computer? _____

3. Third Sentence: She reached in with a pair of tweezers and pulled out a moth.

What did those words make you picture? _____

_____

_____

1. What did you see for tweezers? _____

2. What did you see Grace doing with the tweezers? _____

3. What did you see for her pulling out a moth? _____

4. What did you see for the moth? _____

4. Fourth Sentence: Then the computer started to work fine.

What did those words make you picture? _____

_____

_____

1. What did you see for the computer starting to work? _____

2. What sounds did you hear? _____

3. What did you see Grace doing now? _____

4. What mood did you see for her? _____

5. Fifth Sentence: Since that time, when a problem on a computer is fixed, it is said to be "debugged."

What did those words make you picture? _____

_____

1. What did you see for a computer being fixed now? _____

2. Who did you picture working on it? _____

3. What did you see for a computer being "debugged?" _____

Picture Summary:

Number your images in order.

☐ Grace reached in with a pair of tweezers and pulled out a moth.

☐ Since that time, when a problem on a computer is fixed, it is said to be "debugged."

☐ In 1947, Grace Hopper's computer at Harvard University wasn't working right.

☐ Then the computer started to work fine.

Critical Thinking

Write a Word Summary:

_____
_____
_____
_____

Main Idea:

Check the box that best describes all your images—the main idea.

☐ The term "debugged" began when Grace Hopper removed a moth from a computer.

☐ In 1947, a computer was not working, so Grace Hopper looked inside.

☐ Grace Hopper reached in the computer and pulled out a moth.

HOTS Questions:

1. How do you think Grace felt when the computer stopped working? _____
_____

2. Why do you think she tried to fix it herself? _____
_____

3. Why do you think Grace got some tweezers to help her? _____
_____

4. Why do you think she needed tweezers to pull out the moth? _____
_____

5. How do you think the moth got inside the computer? _____
_____

6. Why do you think people started using the phrase "debugging?" _____
_____

Write a Story

Make up a story about anything you want!

_____

Did you use all the Structure Words in your story? Check each one you used.

What	Size	Color	Mood	Background	Perspective
Number	Shape	Movement	Where	When	Sound

20 Marathon

The marathon race began in 490 B.C. when a soldier was sent to deliver a message over a long distance. The Greek army had won a battle at a town called Marathon. Glad for the victory, the Greek general sent his best runner to Athens with the news. The young man ran in his full armor as fast as he could for the 25 miles it took to get to Athens. When he reached the city, he yelled "Victory!" and then died.

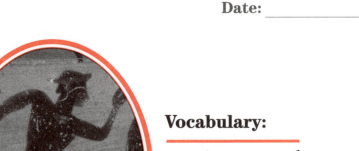

Sentence by Sentence
Date: _____

Vocabulary:

marathon: a race where people run over 26 miles
Greek: a person from Greece, a country in southern Europe
Athens: the capital city of Greece
armor: metal clothes that were worn to protect soldiers

---

1 First Sentence: The marathon race began in 490 B.C. when a soldier was sent to deliver a message over a long distance.

What did those words make you picture? _____

1. What did you see for a marathon race? _____

2. What did you picture for 490 B.C.? _____

3. What did you see for the soldier's uniform? _____

4. What did you see for a message? _____

2 Second Sentence: The Greek army had won a battle at a town called Marathon.

What did those words make you picture? _____

1. What did you see for a Greek army? _____

2. What did you see for a battle? _____

3. What did you see for them winning a battle? _____

4. What did you hear? _____

78

3 Third Sentence: Glad for the victory, the Greek general sent his best runner to Athens with the news.

What did those words make you picture? _____
_____

1. What did you see for the Greek general? _____
_____

2. What did you see for his "best runner?" _____
_____

3. What did you picture for the "news?" _____
_____

4. What did you picture the runner was going to do? _____
_____

4 Fourth Sentence: The young man ran in his full armor as fast as he could for the 25 miles it took to get to Athens.

What did those words make you picture? _____
_____

1. What did you see for armor? _____
_____

2. What did you see for him in his full armor? _____
_____

3. What did you see for him running in his armor? _____
_____

4. What did you see for how long 25 miles is? _____
_____

5 Fifth Sentence: When he reached the city, he yelled "Victory!" and then died.

What did those words make you picture? _____
_____

1. What did you picture for him reaching the city? _____
_____

2. What did he look like now? _____
_____

3. What did you see for him dying? _____
_____

Picture Summary:

Number your images in order.

☐ The Greek army had won a battle at a town called Marathon.

☐ The runner ran in his full armor as fast as he could for the 25 miles it took to get to Athens.

☐ The Greek general sent his best runner to Athens with the news.

☐ When the runner reached the city, he yelled "Victory!" and then died.

Critical Thinking

Write a Word Summary:

_____
_____
_____
_____

Main Idea:

Check the box that best describes all your images—the main idea.

☐ The Greek army won a battle at a town called Marathon.

☐ The marathon race began when a soldier ran 25 miles to deliver a message.

☐ A soldier ran in his full armor as fast as he could all the way to Athens.

HOTS Questions:

1. Why do you think the soldier had to run to deliver the message? _____

2. Why do you think the Greek general wanted to deliver a message about his victory? _____

3. What do you think the best runner might have been like? _____

4. Why do you think the young man ran as fast as he could the entire way to Athens? _____

5. Why do you think the soldier ran while wearing his armor? _____

6. Why do you think we call long races all over the world marathon races? _____

Write a Story

Make up a story about the course of the young runner in this story.

_____
_____
_____
_____
_____
_____
_____
_____
_____
_____
_____
_____
_____
_____
_____
_____
_____

Did you use all the Structure Words in your story? Check each one you used.

What	Size	Color	Mood	Background	Perspective
Number	Shape	Movement	Where	When	Sound

Notes

Analysis of Student Performance:

Notes

Analysis of Student Performance:

Notes

Analysis of Student Performance: